PRAYER SOLUTIONS

REAL TALKS! REAL ISSUES! REAL PRAYERS!

PROPHETESS SHEBA BROWN

ISBN 978-1-365-78066-0

Content ID: 13854488

P.O. Box 1525 Troy, New York 12181
To request permission email: shebatalk@gmail.com

Unless otherwise noted, all scripture quotations are from the King James Version, The Living Bible Copyright ©1971 or Amplified version of the Bible (AMP) Copyright ©2015.

Author: Sheba Brown
Designing Director: Ingrid K. Bennett
Cover Design: Ingrid K. Bennett
Managing Editor: Ingrid K. Bennett

Printed in the United States of America.

PROPHETESS SHEBA BROWN

Prophetess Sheba Brown is the author of 12 books, including soon to be released
"The Prayer Solution" – Real Talks! Real Issues! Real Prayers!

"Sheba Talks" – Real Talks! Real Issues! Real Solutions!

The Facts of King from a Queen's Perspective

and The Design of a Prophetic Champion.

Order her books from Amazon, Barnes & Nobles and Walmart.

To schedule her for Appearances, Speaking Engagements or as a Life Coach please contact QTS Publishing 1-800-290-1276

PRAYER PREFACE

Father, we thank you in the name of Jesus. It is by the power of God that the angels protect us, the angels guide us. FATHER, we thank you now that EVERY ASSIGNMENT is canceled from your people, our families, our children, from the ministry and our relationships! We thank you even as they travel up the highway, down the highway, across the highway at school, at work and throughout the day there is no earth thing that can happen because God, you have already ordained that they shall return back to their places the same way that THEY LEFT it.

FATHER, now we thank you. For them that need healing, they are healed! For them that need deliverance, they are delivered! For them that need a victory they got a victory. For them that's in a storm we command peace in the storm. For whom the Lord has set free is free indeed. It is by the Power of the Holy Ghost that has invested in us/. The angels in heaven are taking charge of us! The angels are for us! The angels will guide us Because you have commanded the angels to take charge over us.

PRAYER BY PROPHETESS SHEBA BROWN

INTRODUCTION

This is Sheba Talks. Yes, Queen Sheba. My talk show is about Real Talks! Real Issues! Real Solutions! One of the solutions that I promote even as a Community Leader, as a Pastor, is I promote PRAYER. I decided this early afternoon that I would come before you and I would begin to pray. The truth of the matter is that sometimes the devil is just busy. He mess' with us, he torments us. The Bible says in the book of John 10:10 that the devil comes to kill, steal and destroy. Today is a day that we will not allow the enemy to destroy. We will not allow him to kill, we will not allow him to steal.

We will use the POWER OF PRAYER to prevail. Psalms 23 declares that the Lord is our Shepherd, we shall not want. Because God is our Shepherd, we are protected by Him, and we are protected by his angels. Rather you bow your head in PRAYER. Rather you look along with me in your Bible, we know that God is about to bless us in this year. This year, 2023, is the YEAR OF THE WINNER! It is the YEAR OF THE MOUTH! It's the year that we open our mouth in PRAYER! It's the year that we open our mouth in worship. It's the year that we open our MOUTH IN VICTORY! I encourage you on today that if you are going through something, PRAYER is the post that you should be on.

THIS IS DECREED AS OUR VICTORY!

The Bible decrees in Jesus' name, FATHER, that no weapon that is formed against us shall prosper, and every tongue that shall arise against us in judgment shall be condemned. I am established in righteousness, and oppression is far from us, according to Isaiah 54:14, God, I thank you that the weapons of our warfare are not carnal, but they are mighty through God by the pulling down of every stronghold according to 2 Corinthians 10:4 I thank you that by your WORD we take the shield of faith and quench every fiery dart of the enemy. According to Ephesians 6:16 FATHER, in the name of Jesus, there are people out there today that are discouraged. They brought discouragement into their year; they brought upset into their year.

The enemy already sent a storm, but according to Ephesians 6:17, we should take the SWORD of the Spirit, which is the WORD of God, and use it against the enemy. FATHER, I thank you that we are REDEEMED from the curse of the law, we are REDEEMED from poverty, we are REDEEMED from sickness. FATHER, in the name of Jesus, according To Galatians, the third chapter, God, I. Thank You, O God, that we shall overcome, because greater is HE that is in us than he that is in the world according to 1 John 4:4. God, I thank you according to Ephesians 6:14-17 that I stand my ground in the day, oh God. Girded up, FATHER, in the name of Jesus, with truth, God, with the breastplate of righteousness, our feet shod with the Gospel of Peace, taking the Shield of

Faith. God, because of that we are covered with the Helmet Of Salvation we use the WORD of God, which is the SWORD of the Spirit, FATHER, to destroy and dismantle every work and every plan of the enemy. FATHER, I thank you that you have delivered us from the powers of darkness and that you have translated us into the KINGDOM of our God, that we have become citizens, God's heirs and joint heirs to your son Jesus Christ.

According to Colossians 1:13 Ephesians I thank you in the name of Jesus, that we do not have the spirit of fear, but of Power, Love And A Sound Mind. We do not have the spirit of anxiety and depression, we do not have the spirit of torment, but FATHER, we have the spirit according to 2 Timothy 1:7. FATHER, in the name of Jesus of POWER, LOVE AND OF a SOUND MIND. God, I thank you that the mind that is stayed on Jesus Christ shall be kept in perfect peace. God, I thank you that we are blessed with all spiritual blessings in heavenly places in Christ Jesus. God, I thank you in the name of Jesus that by your stripes we are HEALED all day long according to Isaiah 53. FATHER, in the name of Jesus, God, I thank you that your hand is upon us, FATHER, and that your hand is upon the neck of our enemies, according to Genesis 49:8

FATHER, I thank that you have anointed us for such a time as this. God, I thank you according to Psalms 23 God, that you anointed our head with oil, FATHER, and that our cup runneth over in Jesus' name. God, I thank you that we walk in light, for there is no darkness in you. In Jesus name, I thank you that every dark situation, every dark circumstance, every dark thing in our life, is delivered. God, it does not matter what is dark in our life, you are the light that exposes our darkness; That healing will take place. FATHER, this represents the righteousness of God. I thank you father, according to Deuteronomy 28:13 that WE ARE THE HEAD AND NOT THE TAIL and we decree that things SHALL BE ESTABLISHED IN OUR LIFE according to the WORD! In the name of Jesus! I thank you because we have favor with God and with Men in the name of Jesus!

According to God and his word in the name of Jesus.

God, I thank you that we will be satisfied, FATHER, with long life. FATHER And That Your Salvation is our portion. God, I thank you, according to Psalms 91, thank you. In the secret place of the Most High shall abide under the shadows of the Almighty. I thank you that you have given us REVELATION and that you have allowed us to be blessed! FATHER, I thank you in the name of Jesus. We are filled with your blessings, FATHER. God, I thank you, in the name of Jesus, FATHER, that you have allowed your hands and your face to shine upon us, FATHER, in the name of Jesus. God, I thank you that you are forgiving us for every sin, FATHER, and that we are blessed in the Lord according to Romans 4:7. I thank you, God, in the name of Jesus. WE ARE CHOSEN AND BLESSED BY YOU.

God, I thank you even according to Your WORD, FATHER, that whatever the enemy is up to, that you have already dismantled his plan. God, I thank you in Jesus' Name, oh, God, that we need you. I thank you, as we cry out to you FATHER that we can't do this without you. I thank you that you make known unto us the mysteries of the Gospel and the mysteries of our FATHER, in the name of Jesus, and that you cause us to understand the WORD of God in your POWER. GOD, AND WE WILL RECEIVE UNLIMITED REVELATION. I thank you that the CHAINS ARE BEING BROKEN off us. I thank you, in the name of

Jesus, that you made our darkness into light, FATHER. I thank you that even the hidden things, FATHER, which are hidden from us, the riches, the revelation of your word oh, even in the secret places are revealed to us, FATHER, that they will now be known to us.

I thank You, O God, that the mouth that had risen against us, oh, God, shall be silent. That the enemy, O God, that accused your people, oh, God, and that speaks against us, FATHER, that their tongue should cleave unto their mouth. I thank you that we bind, and we rebuke ungodly forces, God, in those things that operate against us in Jesus' Name. I bind and rebuke, O God, in the name of Jesus, every weapon, FATHER, that the enemy had sent our way, God, in the Name of Jesus. God,

I thank you that the PRAYER's, of the righteous availed much, and we shall Win and not lose. Hallelujah, FATHER. In the name of Jesus. God, just in Jesus's name I just thought to thank you. God said in the word, I will come in and encourage you in PRAYER and encourage you to believe God, and to encourage you in your healing and to encourage you in your victory and to encourage you in your deliverance, for whom the Lord set FREE is FREE indeed.

This prayer is to encourage you to let you know to just hold on one more day for your tomorrows will come and be your day of victory. God, we thank you that when they're tomorrow come, FATHER, that you will have an open door of blessings. I want you to know that if doors are closing, God will open a window. If things aren't turning around, God would turn around. I know that sometimes we're discouraged and sometimes we feel like God, there's nothing else in the name of Jesus. I want you to be encouraged today and, in your tomorrow's, knowing that God is going to come through for you.

We destroy every assignment off your thoughts. We break every assignment off your thoughts that the enemy planned against you. We destroy every assignment that the devil meant for your evil, that God will work it to your good. We bless the Lord, all our souls and all that is within us. For we run into God because HE IS A REFUGE, and we hide in him. We thank God on today that he has already declared, even according to his WORD, that we shall have the victory. FATHER, we bless your name to those of you that are in, and you that are listening or reading this prayer. I hope that This PRAYER touched you.

PRAYERS ARE PURPOSED TO ENCOURAGE YOU!

This is Queen Sheba, with my talk show "SHEBA TALKS" Real Talk! Real Issues to give you Real Solution! There's some of you with the spirit of heaviness and burdens that are on you coming into the year. It is the presence of the Lord that gives us peace. On today we say that the Peace of the Lord is sure and add no sorrow. Romans 8:28 declares All things will work together for you. God is working things to our good to your good! Understand this, that all things will work together FOR THE GOOD of them that love God. I know that sometimes it looks like things aren't going to get any better. Sometimes it feels like things will not get better. I want you to know today that all things work together. All things will work together.

You think that when people revolt against me as a Pastor, or you that I believe, or you should believe what they said or say. I say God, you're a forgiving God of Anybody that makes a mistake of anybody that does have any type of error, wherever I have errored repentance is always going to bring me and you out according to Psalm 51. There are some of you that you've become stuck because of what people thought about you and because of things said to you. Listen who is man that we should be mindful of them that they should be the rumors over our next move in life? Who are they that we should allow them to say if we're going to be healed or not, successful or not, delivered or not? We're going to be healed in our error, we're going to be healed in our mistakes.

NEW YEAR DECLARATION

This is Queen Sheba. We know that the New Year is coming in and when it gets here. We already know what our purpose is and what our purpose was. It always about God getting Glory out of our Victories. 2022 is going to be gone and 2023 is here. When 2023 comes in, we will then be in a position where we will be able to write off everything that happened in 2022. It's at the end of the year when you do a write off, we will be able to write off some things that happen throughout the year. One of the things that happened throughout the year is that there are some people that are not going to go into the next chapter of our books. The journey for 2023 is to write a new book with new chapters. We are not sad about it. We should be very excited about, yet the next chapter of what God is going to do in our life.

We are all God's children. Although along the way we didn't get along and we didn't make the best decisions. And even in all of that, God is not going to destroy his children. Let me just open by saying this. Just like you feel you can't make it even though you're doing your best and you're going through heart-aching pain, just know that it's only your test and you're going to make it. Believe me what I'm telling you because HE has his hands on you and God will see you through. Don't you give in don’t you dare give up! If people don’t believe in you, Don't You dare Give Up! And Don't you dare Give In! It’s just another battle and you will surely Win. I wanted you to be able to know that 2023 will be the YEAR OF THE BETTER. It is the YEAR OF THE WINNER. The WINNER is the one that has the ability and knows what it will take to be able to know Victory is close. Despite, whatever you're going through in that storm you must find or have found strength within. That way you do not assassinate your next move. You will not fight against or stand against your next journey. Just because you had some trials and tribulations and things of life nature. BE THE WINNER. To all of you that have overcome, those of you that have been triumphant, and those of you that have made your way to a GREAT WIN, WE SAY CONGRATULATIONS! Continue to overcome!

To the next chapter in your book and your next journey we are cheering for you in the years to come that you will FIND YOUR STRENGTH IN YOUR VICTORIES! Take your enemy to high altitudes and suffocate them in the levels that they are not able to survive there.

The enemy is not going to be able to win against you. We celebrate you and we encourage you to know that GREATER IS HE THAT IS IN YOU THAN HE THAT IS IN THE WORLD. We congratulate you. We celebrate you yes, from the Sheba talk show, from the TFM Ministries Inc., to let you know that despite that you did not dot every I or cross every T, that the Lord has a great and awesome plan for you. We celebrate you for the next coming opportunity of greatness that is coming to you as a winner. We celebrate you that you became an overcomer and you're winning. Be a witness that the kingdom and the God in your life allows you to win despite the situation. God will allow you to prevail. Your testimonies of your GREAT VICTORIES concerning the WINS that God gave you are near!

This is the YEAR OF RESTORATION. It is the YEAR OF THE MOUTH, the YEAR THAT THE RIGHTEOUS shall proclaim, that God allowed them to prevail over their enemies! And God allowed them to overcome their storms! And that God allowed them to come through and have peace during their trials. The JOURNEY OF THE WINNER.

BIOGRAPHY

Currently, Apostle Sheba Brown's Godly assignment is to empower and equip God's people with the word of God. God uses her to change the life of his people by encouraging them to Hope and purpose. APOSTLE SHEBA is a strategist when it comes to warfare and dismantling the plan of the kingdom of darkness. She uses compassion insight and revelation from the word of God to touch the hearts of God's people. She has biblical-based principles purposed for healing the body of Christ she engages in spiritual warfare with determination to dismantle the plan of the enemy by cheating the possible and teaching that God achieves the impossible. The body of Christ is impacted by her preaching with demonstration of power reminding the people that they are the head and not the tail.

She was licensed and ordained as a Minister by Bishop Avery Comithier in 1993 who was the Overseer and Pastor of Elijah Missionary Baptist Church at 12 Benjamin St. in Albany. She was also trained and overseen by Reverend Dr. Mini L. Burns of Universal Baptist Church located at 25 Washington St., Saratoga Springs New York. Dr. Burns also Licensed and Ordained her with an Evangelist license. She was consecrated and ordained as an Apostle and confirmed as a Prophet on November 15, 2008. She is the Founder and Senior Pastor of Triumphant Fellowship Ministries, Inc. and Lion Of Judah Ministries, Inc. Since 1998 she currently has two locations one in

Baltimore Maryland and in the Troy NY area. Since COVID-19 all services are held through video conferencing. She is the author of 12 books and several of her books landed in Walmart Amazon Barnes Nobles and Lulu Publishing such as the Spiritual Assassin I'm built for this. Her most recent book that was released is **Sheba Talks. Real Talks! Real Issues! Real Solutions** based on her talk show "Sheba Talks." In addition to overseeing several ministries and counseling Pastors across the country she is an entrepreneur and has a business called City Of Jewels. She is also the mother and manager of 2017 2019 2021 USA National Junior Olympian Jadah Robinson. She currently along with her brother Samuel Bunch have open The Next Bunch

Boxing gym located at the Griswold Heights Community Center in Troy NY. She is a USA level one boxing coach who has been an intricate part of developing a community boxing program to help get youth of the street. She is the founder and chief executive officer of the P&P Rock Initiative Reentry Program they provide services to men and women who are transitioning from incarceration, drug addiction, alcoholism homelessness and rehabilitation. As a part of her concern for the community she manages an employment search program and a community service program to assist men and women who have been charged with misdemeanors and felonies. She also has the Toys for Tots program to give toys to families where there are single parents and parents who are incarcerated or who have issues with drugs and alcohol. She also manages an annual Turkey drive program for families during the Thanksgiving season. The programs that she oversees are purposed to help the needs of the communities that have issues with drug infestation and are crime ridden. She recently launched The Word Table Talk show where panelists talk about hot topic social issues and relationship concerns the show, along with prayers and Bible studies can be watched on APOSTLE SHEBA Brown's YouTube channel SHEBA TALKS - THE WORD TABLE TALK. She is a motivational speaker and a preacher after God's own heart being called to move the assignment of demonic forces by using the word of God commanding the yolk of the devil to be destroyed off the neck of God's people. She also motivates one to operate in the spirit of excellence that they may fulfill their assignment by operating on purpose passion and power. Her prophetic gift operates like Elijah with accuracy. She is also the Founder of the School of the Prophets where the first semester was launched in 2014 using her Prophetic Manual to enhance and educate those who operate in the Office of the Prophet. She has received divine and sovereign orders from the King of Kings that she must carry out.

www.ingramcontent.com/pod-product-compliance
Ingram Content Group UK Ltd.
Pitfield, Milton Keynes, MK11 3LW, UK
UKHW020137250726
13967UKWH00002B/707

9 781365 780660